W9-DEU-520

★

THIS JOURNAL BELONGS TO

DATE

★

Peace in the middle of a war zone is unthinkable—
until we turn to God—and then it settles joyfully over our minds and hearts.

EDIE MELSON

★

Many of us have sent someone we love off to war and were left with our own battles to fight: loneliness, fear, worry, and more. When we feel helpless, we can take our fears to the One who holds the universe in His hands and loves us more than anything. This journal is just a starting point to help you find your own voice as you call out on behalf of the one you love.

Blessings,

Edie Melson

★

HOW TO USE THIS JOURNAL

This journal is for anyone who cares for a soldier—parents, friends, spouses, children, grandparents. Two sections are provided: "Prayers for My Soldier" and "Prayers for Me." The pronouns change from prayer to prayer to represent both men and women serving in the military. We suggest inserting your soldier's name in place of the pronouns to make it more personal and meaningful.

★

PRAYERS FOR MY SOLDIER

HELP MY SOLDIER MAKE WISE DECISIONS

★

Dear Lord, I know at times he has to make
life-and-death decisions in a split second.
Please give him the information he needs to choose wisely.
Amen.

I declare the end from the beginning, and from long ago what is not yet done, saying: My plan will take place, and I will do all My will.

ISAIAH 46:10 HCSB

Be faithful in small things, because it is in them that your strength lies.

MOTHER TERESA

GIVE MY SOLDIER A CLEAR HEAD

★

Dear Lord, protect my soldier from confusion and distraction.
Let him see into the heart of any person who approaches him.
Give him the foresight he needs to anticipate obstacles.
Amen.

If any of you lacks wisdom, you should ask God, who gives generously to all without finding fault, and it will be given to you.

JAMES 1:5 NIV

One who gains strength by overcoming obstacles
possesses the only strength which can overcome adversity.

ALBERT SCHWEITZER

HELP MY LOVED ONE CHOOSE JOY

★

Dear Lord, let my loved one choose joy. Let joy bubble up from deep inside, and make it contagious. No one rejoices in war, but You can bring beauty to light wherever she is.
Amen.

You, Lord, keep my lamp burning; my God turns my darkness into light.

PSALM 18:28 NIV

Joy does not simply happen to us.
We have to choose joy and keep choosing it every day.

HENRI J. M. NOUWEN

GIVE MY SOLDIER TOOLS TO DEAL WITH FEAR

★

Dear Lord, when waves of fear wash over my soldier,
be there to catch him. Show him how precious he is to You.
Replace his fear with peace as You wrap him in Your love.
Amen.

God has made us what we are. In Christ Jesus, God made us to do good works, which God planned in advance for us to live our lives doing.

EPHESIANS 2:10 NCV

Fear always springs from ignorance.

RALPH WALDO EMERSON

GRANT MY SOLDIER YOUR PERSPECTIVE

★

Dear Lord, open my soldier's eyes so he can see You at work.
Let him catch a glimpse of Your plan.
Show him that what he's doing has meaning and makes a difference.
Amen.

And to man He said, "Behold, the fear of the Lord, that is wisdom, and to depart from evil is understanding."

JOB 28:28 NKJV

The only true wisdom is in knowing you know nothing.

SOCRATES

KEEP MY SOLDIER GROUNDED IN YOUR TRUTH

★

Dear Lord, show my soldier—in concrete, physical ways—
that Your character isn't in conflict with what he's experiencing.
Show him the relevance of Your Word to what is going on around him.
Amen.

Sanctify them by the truth; your word is truth.

JOHN 17:17 NIV

The truth does not change according to our ability to stomach it.

FLANNERY O'CONNOR

GOD, PLEASE INTERVENE FOR MY SOLDIER

★

Dear Lord, intervene for my loved one and help him to focus on the job at hand. Give him peace about his loved ones at home. Surround him with a hedge of protection.
Amen.

Be very careful, then, how you live—not as unwise but as wise.

EPHESIANS 5:15 NIV

Habits are first cobwebs, then cables. The chains of habit are too weak to be felt until they are too strong to be broken.

SAMUEL JOHNSON

HELP MY LOVED ONE SEE GOD AT WORK

★

Dear Lord, let my loved one see glimpses of the way You work.
Keep him actively looking for You everywhere,
and then let him find You in the most unlikely places.
Amen.

I love those who love me, and those who seek me find me.

PROVERBS 8:17 NIV

Perfect goodness can never debate about the end to be attained,
and perfect wisdom cannot debate about the means most suited to achieve it.

C. S. LEWIS

GIVE MY LOVED ONE COURAGE

★

Dear Lord, let the fear my loved one encounters protect him from danger, but never let it hinder him when courage is needed. Show him that continuing on is the mark of true courage.
Amen.

Have I not commanded you? Be strong and of good courage; do not be afraid, nor be dismayed, for the LORD your God is with you wherever you go.

JOSHUA 1:9 NKJV

If we desire our faith to be strengthened, we should not shrink from opportunities where our faith may be tried, and therefore, through trial, be strengthened.

GEORGE MÜLLER

STRENGTHEN MY SOLDIER'S PRAYER LIFE

★

Dear Lord, keep my soldier centered on You and on Your plan for his life. Help him become so familiar with Your voice that he recognizes You in the mightiest roar or the tiniest whispered breeze. Amen.

Therefore I want the men everywhere to pray, lifting up holy hands without anger or disputing.

1 TIMOTHY 2:8 NIV

God speaks to all individuals through what happens to them moment by moment.

J. P. DE CAUSSADE

GIVE MY SOLDIER TIME TO LAUGH

★

Dear Lord, give my soldier plenty of opportunities to relax and have fun while he's away. Surround him with good friends who can help him shake off the stress and worry.
Amen.

*For the kingdom of God is not eating and drinking,
but righteousness and peace and joy in the Holy Spirit.*

ROMANS 14:17 NASB

Life is worth living as long as there's a laugh in it.

L. M. MONTGOMERY

KEEP MY LOVED ONE'S HOPE ALIVE

★

Dear lord, please give my loved one reasons to stay hopeful.
Put things and people around her to raise her spirits and restore her hope.
Remind her that she has a purpose—for good and not evil.
Amen.

A man's steps are established by the LORD, and He takes pleasure in his way. Though he falls, he will not be overwhelmed, because the LORD holds his hand.

PSALM 37:23–24 HCSB

It is often in the darkest skies that we see the brightest stars.

RICHARD PAUL EVANS

KEEP MY SOLDIER SPIRITUALLY STRONG

★

Dear Lord, provide the perfect rest when my loved one is so tired. Grant him perfect peace when he's emotionally exhausted. Comfort him through others, through Your Word, and through our prayers. Amen.

It is God who arms me with strength and keeps my way secure.

2 SAMUEL 22:33 NIV

In the depth of winter, I finally learned that within me
there lay an invincible summer.

ALBERT CAMUS

GIVE MY LOVED ONE PHYSICAL STRENGTH

★

Dear Lord, equip my loved one to stay physically healthy. You are the creator and designer of our bodies, and You know how to best care for us. Keep his body healthy and bring him home safe. Amen.

You armed me with strength for battle; you humbled my adversaries before me.

PSALM 18:39 NIV

The strength of a man consists in finding out the way in which God is going, and going in that way too.

HENRY WARD BEECHER

GIVE MY SOLDIER INNER STRENGTH

★

Dear Lord, grant my soldier the kind of courage only You can provide.
Remind her that who she is never changes,
and even more importantly, who You are, God, never changes.
Amen.

Surely God is my salvation; I will trust and not be afraid. The L*ORD*,
the L*ORD himself, is my strength and my defense; he has become my salvation.*

ISAIAH 12:2 NIV

Be sure you put your feet in the right place; then stand firm.

ABRAHAM LINCOLN

YOU ARE STRONGER THAN ANY ENEMY

★

Dear Lord, when we call on You, our enemies melt before You. None can stand against One so great as You. Our enemies are blind to the power of love. I pray You remind my soldier of this. Amen.

On the day I called, You answered me; You made me bold with strength in my soul.

PSALM 138:3 NASB

Don't magnify your problems, magnify your God.... He's got you covered.

TONY EVANS

BE MY SOLDIER'S SECURITY

★

Dear Lord, please be my loved one's security. There are times when he feels so lost and alone. Put people around him who can remind him of Your love and constant care. Amen.

The works of His hands are truth and justice; all His instructions are trustworthy.

PSALM 111:7 HCSB

Peace comes in situations completely surrendered to the sovereign authority of Christ.

BETH MOORE

YOU ARE WORTHY OF OUR FAITH

★

Dear Lord, You are faithful and true. You are worthy of our faith. You never leave us alone to fend for ourselves. No matter how deep the valley of the shadow of death, You are always beside us. Amen.

I called to the L*ORD, who is worthy of praise, and have been saved from my enemies.*

2 SAMUEL 22:4 NIV

The secret of the mystery is: God is always greater.
No matter how great we think Him to be, His love is always greater.

BRENNAN MANNING

GIVE MY SOLDIER THE FAITH TO MAKE IT THROUGH

★

Dear Lord, my soldier in the midst of war desperately needs faith to make it through, and so do I. Give him what he needs to fight the battle over despair and come out the other side victorious. Amen.

Yet those who wait for the LORD will gain new strength; they will mount up with wings like eagles, they will run and not get tired, they will walk and not become weary.

ISAIAH 40:31 NASB

Faith is confidence in the veracity of what God has said.

LARRY HUGGINS

GIVE MY SOLDIER WHAT SHE NEEDS TO STAY FAITHFUL

★

Dear Lord, let my loved one see You today. She's in the middle of miserable circumstances and must be weary of all she sees. She needs the encouragement that only Your presence can bring. Amen.

But the Lord is faithful, and He will strengthen and protect you from the evil one.

2 THESSALONIANS 3:3 NASB

All I have seen teaches me to trust the Creator for all I have not seen.

RALPH WALDO EMERSON

WRAP MY SOLDIER IN YOUR LOVE AND CARE

★

Dear Lord, remind my loved one of how precious he is to You. I know You love him even more than I do. Wrap him so tightly in Your love that he can't help but know You're there. Amen.

The Lord is righteous in all his ways and faithful in all he does.

PSALM 145:17 NIV

Though our feelings come and go, God's love for us does not.

C. S. LEWIS

GIVE MY SOLDIER THE COURAGE TO BELIEVE

★

Dear Lord, give my soldier the courage to believe You in spite of the circumstances. Let him witness acts of kindness and love. Show him You value his sacrifice and that You will never abandon him. Amen.

Wait for the LORD; be strong and take heart and wait for the LORD.

PSALM 27:14 NIV

True faith means holding nothing back.
It means putting every hope in God's fidelity to His promises.

FRANCIS CHAN

SHOW MY SOLDIER YOUR LOVE IN THE HARD PLACES

★

Dear Lord, my loved one is in a hard place. Guard his heart. I believe You can protect him from emotional injury just as easily as physical. Show him Your love in the hard places. Amen.

God, who has called you into fellowship with his Son, Jesus Christ our Lord, is faithful.

1 CORINTHIANS 1:9 NCV

He persists in loving us with unending, outrageous love.

FRANCIS CHAN

LET MY LOVED ONE SEE YOU WALKING BESIDE HIM

★

Dear Lord, show my soldier how You're working all around him. Give him opportunities for positive, life-building work. Show him the effect he can have on people when he stays close to You. Amen.

The Lord replied, "My Presence will go with you, and I will give you rest."

EXODUS 33:14 NIV

Faith is taking the first step, even when you don't see the whole staircase.

MARTIN LUTHER KING JR.

HELP MY LOVED ONE TRUST GOD'S CHARACTER

★

Dear Lord, give my loved one a glimpse of Your perfect plan, the way You bring good out of a horrible situation. Don't allow bitterness to take root. Instead, heal her and give her the answers she needs. Amen.

Make sure that no one falls short of the grace of God and that no root of bitterness springs up, causing trouble and by it, defiling many.

HEBREWS 12:15 HCSB

When trouble comes, focus on God's ability to care for you.

CHARLES STANLEY

TEACH MY SOLDIER TO RELY ON YOU

★

Dear Lord, my soldier's training showed him how to rely on himself, his comrades, and his commanders. Teach him also how to rely on You. Become his foundation that will never shift, shake, or collapse. Amen.

But seek first his kingdom and his righteousness,
and all these things will be given to you as well.

MATTHEW 6:33 NIV

There are no "ifs" in God's world. And no places that are safer than other places. The center of His will is our only safety—let us pray that we may always know it!

CORRIE TEN BOOM

PROTECT MY SOLDIER AS HE LEAVES FOR WAR

★

Dear Lord, protect my loved one as he travels to the places he'll be stationed. Go before him and make his way there safe. Keep him from harm as he settles in, and then bring him back home safely. Amen.

The L*ORD* *himself goes before you and will be with you; he will never leave you nor forsake you. Do not be afraid; do not be discouraged.*

DEUTERONOMY 31:8 NIV

Basically, there are two paths you can walk: faith or fear.
It's impossible to simultaneously trust God and not trust God.

CHARLES STANLEY

BE MY SOLDIER'S SHIELD

★

Dear Lord, keep my loved one close to You. Guard his mind, and when necessary be a shield, keeping him from all that would harm him. Help his heart to become more like Yours. Amen.

You, Lord, are a shield around me, my glory, the One who lifts my head high.

PSALM 3:3 NIV

Anything under God's control is never out of control.

CHARLES R. SWINDOLL

PROTECT MY SOLDIER FROM BECOMING BITTER

★

Dear Lord, please protect my soldier from becoming angry or bitter. Keep him safe spiritually and emotionally. Let him see how You are using him to make a positive difference in the world. Amen.

Get rid of all bitterness, rage and anger, brawling and slander, along with every form of malice.

EPHESIANS 4:31 NIV

Bitterness imprisons life; love releases it.

HARRY EMERSON FOSDICK

PROTECT MY SOLDIER FROM HER ENEMIES

★

Dear Lord, protect my loved one. Let her see the hidden dangers in her path. Guard those around her, and protect them as well. Confuse the enemy, and let their plans fall to pieces.
Amen.

In God I have put my trust, I shall not be afraid. What can man do to me?

PSALM 56:11 NASB

Worry is a cycle of inefficient thoughts whirling around a center of fear.

CORRIE TEN BOOM

GUARD MY SOLDIER'S REST

★

Dear Lord, guard my soldier's rest. Make sure he gets enough sleep to stay focused during the day. Grant him deep sleep that renews his mind. Wherever he lays his head, be there with Your peace.
Amen.

Those who go to God Most High for safety will be protected by the Almighty.

PSALM 91:1 NCV

Every outcome of every challenge should reveal how God supplies the grace to make it through the seemingly impossible.

LEO PATALINGHUG

PROTECT MY LOVED ONE FROM TROUBLE

★

Dear Lord, keep my loved one away from trouble. Keep him from others who don't think before they act. Watch over him as he goes about his duties and especially as he fills his free time. Amen.

I waited patiently for the LORD; he turned to me and heard my cry.
He lifted me out of the slimy pit, out of the mud and mire;
he set my feet on a rock and gave me a firm place to stand.

PSALM 40:1–2 NIV

Talk we will of faith, if we do not trust and rely upon Him, we do not believe in Him.

ANTHONY FARINDON

GO BEFORE MY SOLDIER

★

Dear Lord, as a soldier, my loved one will not consider himself when someone else is in danger, and I know that is why he is a good soldier. Go before him and cover him with Your protection. Amen.

You are my hiding place; you will protect me from trouble and surround me with songs of deliverance.

PSALM 32:7 NIV

A man of courage is also full of faith.

MARCUS TULLIUS CICERO

MAKE MY SOLDIER'S TRANSITION IN-COUNTRY EASY

★

Dear Lord, help my soldier make the transition to her new environment. May the time change not exhaust her or the new food upset her system. Give her things that are familiar and remind her of home. Amen.

The LORD will watch over your coming and going both now and forevermore.

PSALM 121:8 NIV

We aren't just thrown on this earth like dice tossed across a table.
We are lovingly placed here for a purpose.

CHARLES R. SWINDOLL

GUARD MY LOVED ONE'S MIND

★

Dear Lord, guard my loved one's mind. Keep him safe from any emotional, psychological, and spiritual damage. Let his mind be at peace and know that You're in control—no matter what. Amen.

He will call on me, and I will answer him;
I will be with him in trouble, I will deliver him and honor him.

PSALM 91:15 NIV

For happiness one needs security, but joy can spring like a flower even from the cliffs of despair.

ANNE MORROW LINDBERGH

TEACH MY LOVED ONE TO PRAY

★

Dear Lord, teach my loved one how to have an ongoing conversation with You, and let her learn to recognize Your voice even in chaos. Make her so tuned in to You that she can hear Your tiniest whisper. Amen.

He was praying in a certain place, and when He finished, one of His disciples said to Him, "Lord, teach us to pray, just as John also taught his disciples."

LUKE 11:1 HCSB

Prayer is not asking. Prayer is putting oneself in the hands of God, at His disposition, and listening to His voice in the depth of our hearts.

MOTHER TERESA

FINDING PEACE IN THE MIDST OF WAR

★

Dear Lord, when my loved one runs into things that don't make sense, give her confirmation of Your abiding love. Show her just how powerful You are by providing peace in the midst of war. Amen.

Now may the Lord of peace Himself give you peace always in every way. The Lord be with you all.

2 THESSALONIANS 3:16 NKJV

Like a spring of pure water, God's peace in our hearts brings cleansing and refreshment to our minds and bodies.

BILLY GRAHAM

GRANT MY SOLDIER AND HIS COMPANIONS A SABBATH REST

★

Dear Lord, remind my soldier and his companions that in You can be found a peace that passes all understanding. Refresh each of them as they partake of fellowship with You and with each other.
Amen.

So there is still a Sabbath rest for God's people.

HEBREWS 4:9 NIRV

As sure as ever God puts His children in the furnace,
He will be in the furnace with them.

CHARLES SPURGEON

REASSURE MY SOLDIER

★

Dear Lord, I know my soldier must feel trapped by circumstances that are beyond his control. Please show him they are not beyond Your control. Reassure him that You're all he needs.
Amen.

Therefore, my dear brothers, be steadfast, immovable, always excelling in the Lord's work, knowing that your labor in the Lord is not in vain.

1 CORINTHIANS 15:58 HCSB

Cleverness is cheap. It is faith that He praises.

GEORGE MACDONALD

THANK YOU FOR THE PEACE YOU PROVIDE

★

Dear Lord, Your peace isn't found in a cessation of war. It's found in a person. When we know Your Son, we know the Author of peace. Remind my soldier of these things.
Amen.

The LORD *gives His people strength; the* LORD *blesses His people with peace.*

PSALM 29:11 HCSB

When it is dark enough, you can see the stars.

RALPH WALDO EMERSON

GRANT MY SOLDIER PEACE WHEN SHE'S EXHAUSTED

★

Dear Lord, as my soldier's circumstances go from one extreme to another, so do her emotions. Protect her from exhaustion and the despair that often comes with it. Let her feel Your peace. Amen.

Cast all your anxiety on him because he cares for you.

1 PETER 5:7 NIV

Peace with God is where all peace begins.

JIM GALLERY

DON'T EVER LET THE LONELINESS BECOME TOO MUCH

★

Dear Lord, give my loved one proof that he has not been forgotten by those at home. Overwhelm him with letters and packages. When he aches for home, replace that longing with the warmth of Your love. Amen.

All my longings lie open before you, Lord; my sighing is not hidden from you.

PSALM 38:9 NIV

We need never shout across the spaces to an absent God.
He is nearer than our own soul, closer than our most secret thoughts.

A. W. TOZER

WITH YOU I KNOW WE HAVE NOTHING TO FEAR

★

Dear Lord, You are our defender, able to protect us from any enemy. You are everywhere, in every time. As my soldier is fighting half a world away, I know there is no reason to fear. Remind my loved one of this. Amen.

So we say with confidence, "The Lord is my helper; I will not be afraid. What can mere mortals do to me?"

HEBREWS 13:6 NIV

Be assured, if you walk with Him and look to Him and expect help from Him, He will never fail you.

GEORGE MÜLLER

GIVE MY LOVED ONE STRONG FRIENDSHIPS

★

Dear Lord, provide my loved one with strong friendships that help him grow in his knowledge of You. Bind them together with love for You. Then give them the courage to share and reach out to others. Amen.

Two are better than one because they have a good return for their labor.

ECCLESIASTES 4:9 NASB

There can be no friendship without confidence,
and no confidence without integrity.

SAMUEL JOHNSON

GIVE MY SOLDIER'S COMMANDERS WISDOM

★

Dear Lord, bless those who are in command over my soldier. Make them aware of the needs of those serving under them. Even in their strength, give them hearts of compassion. Most of all give them hearts focused on You. Amen.

Remember your leaders, who spoke the word of God to you. Consider the outcome of their way of life and imitate their faith.

HEBREWS 13:7 NIV

Take time to deliberate; but when the time for action arrives,
stop thinking and go in.

ANDREW JACKSON

SURROUND MY LOVED ONE WITH A GROUP OF BELIEVERS

★

Dear Lord, create a small pocket of Your kingdom right where
my loved one is. Provide friends who have the same values and beliefs.
Help them gather for worship and prayer.
Amen.

*And let us not give up meeting together. Some are in the habit of doing this.
Instead, let us encourage one another with words of hope.
Let us do this even more as you see Christ's return approaching.*

HEBREWS 10:25 NIRV

No friendship is an accident.

O. HENRY

DON'T LET MY SOLDIER WORRY ABOUT THOSE AT HOME

★

Dear Lord, I know my loved one feels torn between the duty she's committed to and taking care of us. Give her the assurance that she needs to focus wholly on the job she has to do. Amen.

Anxiety in a man's heart weighs it down, but a good word makes it glad.

PROVERBS 12:25 NASB

Do not anticipate trouble or worry about what may never happen.
Keep in the sunlight.

BENJAMIN FRANKLIN

BLESS THE FRIENDS MY LOVED ONE LEFT BEHIND

★

Dear Lord, I know the close friends my loved one left behind worry about her and want to reach out and help, but many aren't sure how. Give them what they need to be able to support her while she's away. Amen.

Therefore comfort one another with these words.

1 THESSALONIANS 4:18 NASB

However rare true love may be, it is less so than true friendship.

ALBERT EINSTEIN

HELP MY SOLDIER BE A FRIEND TO THOSE IN NEED

★

Dear Lord, I'm praying for my loved one to have a heart to see those who need a true friend. And provide him with friends to fill the empty hours. Help them encourage each other and hold each other accountable. Amen.

He who walks with wise men will be wise,
but the companion of fools will suffer harm.

PROVERBS 13:20 NASB

A true friend [discloses] freely, advises justly, assists readily, adventures boldly, takes all patiently, defends courageously, and continues a friend unchangeably.

WILLIAM PENN

RELIEVE MY LOVED ONE OF FINANCIAL WORRIES BACK HOME

★

Dear Lord, provide for my soldier's family in such a visible and abundant way that he won't have to worry. Show him, by providing for his family, how much You honor his sacrifice and his obedience.
Amen.

Every good gift and every perfect gift is from above, and comes down from the Father of lights, with whom there is no variation or shadow of turning.

JAMES 1:17 NKJV

Worry divides the mind.

MAX LUCADO

GIVE MY SOLDIER FREEDOM TO WORSHIP YOU

★

Dear Lord, it's becoming more difficult for my loved one to feel comfortable as a believer in today's military. Protect him and don't let those around him stop him from sharing Your great love and peace. Amen.

And now, Lord, listen to their threats. Lord, help us, your servants, to speak your word without fear.

ACTS 4:29 NCV

You may go through difficulty, hardship, or trial—
but as long as you are anchored to Him, you will have hope.

CHARLES STANLEY

THANK YOU FOR MY LOVED ONE'S FAMILY

★

Dear Lord, thank You for my soldier's loving family.
They support his decision to serve in so many ways.
While he's far away, let them see the good that's coming out of this.
Amen.

Children are a heritage from the Lord, *offspring a reward from him.*

PSALM 127:3 NIV

Our "safe place" is not where we live; it is in whom we live.

TOM WHITE

USE THE FRIENDS OF MY LOVED ONE TO ENCOURAGE HER

★

Dear Lord, I know my soldier has friends to help watch her back in battle, as well as when she's at rest. Use their friendship to spur each other on to great things. Amen.

As iron sharpens iron, so a man sharpens the countenance of his friend.

PROVERBS 27:17 NKJV

Words are easy, like the wind; faithful friends are hard to find.

WILLIAM SHAKESPEARE

PRAYERS FOR ME

STAYING STRONG

★

Dear Lord, help me feel Your presence as I struggle to stay strong while my loved one is away. Bring someone into my life who has struggled with this and overcome it. I need to see that victory is possible.
Amen.

I will not fear though tens of thousands assail me on every side.

PSALM 3:6 NIV

The only way to learn strong faith is to endure great trials.

CHARLES MÜLLER

GIVE ME REST FROM MY FEARS

★

Dear Lord, please intervene and give me the rest I need from my fears. Help me believe that You are taking care of the one I love so dearly. You are my strength, and I'm choosing right now to trust You. Amen.

There is no fear in love. But perfect love drives out fear, because fear has to do with punishment. The one who fears is not made perfect in love.

1 JOHN 4:18 NIV

In the center of a hurricane there is absolute peace and quiet.
There is no safer place than in the center of the will of God.

CORRIE TEN BOOM

THANK YOU THAT YOU ARE A GOD WHO NEVER RESTS

★

Dear Lord, no matter what we're facing we can be at peace with You near. Even now I can picture You watching my soldier as he sleeps. With You always on guard, he can get the rest he needs. Amen.

He will not allow your foot to slip; He who keeps you will not slumber.

PSALM 121:3 NASB

We can be tired, weary, and emotionally distraught, but after spending time alone with God, we find that He injects into our bodies energy, power, and strength.

CHARLES STANLEY

YOUR PERFECT PEACE

★

Dear Lord, give me peace. Teach me how to move beyond the fear.
Use this time to grow my faith and make me into someone
who takes everything to You in prayer.
Amen.

When anxiety was great within me, your consolation brought me joy.

PSALM 94:19 NIV

Worrying does not empty tomorrow of its troubles; it empties today of its strength.

CORRIE TEN BOOM

HELP ME CONTINUE TO MOVE FORWARD

★

Dear Lord, while I'm waiting for my loved one, don't let me waste time. Give me the eyes to see the path You want me to take. Help me look beyond my circumstances. I know You have a purpose for me. Amen.

People may make plans in their minds, but the LORD decides what they will do.

PROVERBS 16:9 NCV

If we only have the will to walk, then God is pleased with our stumbles.

C. S. LEWIS

RESTORE MY SENSE OF FUN

★

Dear Lord, help me recapture that sense of fun I used to have, even when someone I love is far away. Don't let my loved one be afraid to share the times of joy he's experiencing while he's away. Amen.

You will go out in joy and be led forth in peace; the mountains and hills will burst into song before you, and all the trees of the field will clap their hands.

ISAIAH 55:12 NIV

A little faith will bring your soul to heaven,
but a lot of faith will bring heaven to your soul.

DWIGHT L. MOODY

FILL ME UP WITH HOPE

★

Dear Lord, fill me with hope during this time. Put people around me who have been through this and come out victorious. Keep my eyes firmly on You. I am choosing to put my hope in You. Amen.

Rejoice in hope; be patient in affliction; be persistent in prayer.

ROMANS 12:12 HCSB

God is the only One who can make the valley of trouble a door of hope.

CATHERINE MARSHALL

PATIENCE FOR MY LOVED ONE'S RETURN

★

Dear Lord, I'm so tired of waiting for my loved one to come home.
Give me the ability to cope with the time that's left.
Help me find ways to occupy my mind, and keep me focused on You.
Amen.

Even before they call, I will answer; while they are still speaking, I will hear.

ISAIAH 65:24 HCSB

Patience is the ability to idle your motor when you feel like stripping your gears.

BARBARA JOHNSON

LET ME CLING TO YOU

★

Dear Lord, give me a tangible way to know You're listening.
Please strengthen my faith. Show me how to pray when I have no words.
Remind me of Your faithfulness, even when I'm weak.
Amen.

In the same way, the Spirit helps us in our weakness. We do not know what we ought to pray for, but the Spirit himself intercedes for us through wordless groans.

ROMANS 8:26 NIV

Sorrow looks back. Worry looks around. Faith looks up.

RALPH WALDO EMERSON

HELP ME WITH THE SMALL STUFF

★

Dear Lord, some days the small details of life overwhelm me.
Be there for me. Give me the knowledge I need to handle all of this.
Show me when I can do something myself or when I need to ask for help.
Amen.

Let us not grow weary while doing good,
for in due season we shall reap if we do not lose heart.

GALATIANS 6:9 NKJV

By perseverance the snail reached the ark.

CHARLES H. SPURGEON

GROW MY FAITH

★

Dear Lord, I want to be strong for my family and especially for my soldier, but I know I can't until I learn to lean on You. Teach me to turn to You in all my situations.
Amen.

Therefore, do not throw away your confidence, which has a great reward.

HEBREWS 10:35 NASB

Faith is like an empty, open hand stretched out towards God, with nothing to offer and everything to receive.

JOHN CALVIN

THANK YOU THAT YOU HEAR AND ANSWER OUR PRAYERS

★

Dear Lord, You are faithful to care about the people and the things I care about. I can bring You my burdens and lay them at Your feet. I can leave them there, knowing that You will take care of each one. Amen.

Therefore I say to you, whatever things you ask when you pray, believe that you receive them, and you will have them.

MARK 11:24 NKJV

We serve a God who is waiting to hear from you, and He can't wait to respond.

PRISCILLA SHIRER

GIVE ME THE FAITH I NEED TO STAND FIRM

★

Dear Lord, help me release my soldier's protection into Your loving hands. Give me the courage to have faith in You. I'm choosing now to believe You are there with her. Give me the faith to stand firm. Amen.

You, therefore, my son, be strong in the grace that is in Christ Jesus.

2 TIMOTHY 2:1 HCSB

Faith is not belief without proof, but trust without reservation.

ELTON TRUEBLOOD

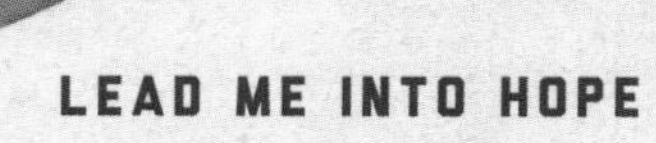

LEAD ME INTO HOPE

★

Dear Lord, I'm tired of living with the fear of what might happen. I need You to replace it with hope. You promise us that hope is found in You. Hold me close, give me Your peace, and lead me to Your hope. Amen.

Trust in the LORD with all your heart, and lean not on your own understanding; in all your ways acknowledge Him, and He shall direct your paths.

PROVERBS 3:5–6 NKJV

Hope is faith in seed form—faith is hope in final form.

REX ROUIS

CARRY ME WHEN I'M WEAK

★

Dear Lord, the Bible promises that when we cry out You are faithful to answer us. Show me the way back to hope. And when I come out of this victorious, help me tell others how You helped me. Amen.

In their misery they cried out to the LORD, and he saved them from their troubles.

PSALM 107:28 NCV

I am mended by my sickness, enriched by my poverty,
and strengthened by my weakness.

ABRAHAM WRIGHT

HELP ME TAKE CARE OF MY HEALTH

★

Dear Lord, I'm praying for my own strength as I wait for my loved one to come home from war. Help me stay focused on keeping myself healthy. Give me the strength to make wise choices.
Amen.

He sent His word and healed them, and delivered them from their destructions.

PSALM 107:20 NASB

It is important to get out of your own way.

RAY BRADBURY

LEND ME YOUR STRENGTH

★

Dear Lord, I'm worn out. I'm exhausted by the worry and fear. Help me turn my focus back to You. Help me once again to find joy in day-to-day life. Replace my fear with peace, and keep me from worry. Amen.

The Lord is my strength and song, and He has become my salvation; this is my God, and I will praise Him; my father's God, and I will extol Him.

EXODUS 15:2 NASB

Courage is resistance to fear, mastery of fear—not absence of fear.

MARK TWAIN

TAKE AWAY MY ANGER AT THE ENEMY

★

Dear Lord, You've promised to teach me to love the unlovable.
When I see someone who reminds me of the enemy,
I want to lash out. Teach me how to return their hatred with love.
Let me see these people as You do.
Amen.

A hot-tempered man stirs up strife, but the slow to anger calms a dispute.

PROVERBS 15:18 NASB

Snuggle in God's arms. When you are hurting, when you feel lonely, left out...
let him cradle you, comfort you, reassure you of His all-sufficient power and love.

KAY ARTHUR

TAKE AWAY MY ANGER AT YOU

★

Dear Lord, I'm mad at You. You are all-powerful; I know You could put an end to this. I also know that You love each of us deeply. Forgive me for my feelings, and help me move past them. Amen.

God, create a clean heart for me and renew a steadfast spirit within me.

PSALM 51:10 HCSB

Past tears are present strength.

GEORGE MACDONALD

HELP ME CHANNEL MY ANGER INTO SOMETHING GOOD

★

Dear Lord, give me the tools I need to let go of my destructive emotions. Replace them with some real, constructive things I can do to make a difference. Show me how to return love when I'm faced with hate. Amen.

Refrain from anger and turn from wrath; do not fret—it leads only to evil.

PSALM 37:8 NIV

For every minute you remain angry, you give up sixty seconds of peace of mind.

RALPH WALDO EMERSON

LEAD ME TO HELP OTHERS

★

Dear Lord, direct me to other people who are struggling with loved ones deployed, and give me the opportunity to reach out to them. Lead others to me so we can support each other and pray together. Amen.

Your word is a lamp for my feet, a light on my path.

PSALM 119:105 NIV

Alone we can do so little; together we can do so much.

HELEN KELLER

I DON'T KNOW HOW TO BE STRONG

★

Dear Lord, show me how to continue on with life and still honor my loved one's service and sacrifice. I feel like I'm caught between two polar opposites. Give me Your perspective and Your wisdom on how to be strong while he is away. Amen.

Splendor and majesty are before Him; strength and joy are in His place.

1 CHRONICLES 16:27 NASB

Deny your weakness and you will never realize God's strength in you.

JONI EARECKSON TADA

LESSON LEARNED

★

Dear Lord, You have been so patient and so loving; use me to be those things for others who are hurting. Never let me forget that You are always with me, no matter the circumstances. Amen.

I pray that the fellowship of your faith may become effective through the knowledge of every good thing which is in you for Christ's sake.

PHILEMON 1:6 NASB

Fellowship is a place of grace, where mistakes aren't rubbed in but rubbed out.
Fellowship happens when mercy wins over justice.

RICK WARREN

Ellie Claire® Gift & Paper Expressions
Franklin, TN 37067
EllieClaire.com
Ellie Claire is registered trademark of Worthy Media, Inc.

Published by Ellie Claire, an imprint of Worthy Publishing Group, a division of Worthy Media, Inc.

ISBN 978-1-63326-102-0

Stock or custom editions of Ellie Claire titles may be purchased in bulk for educational, business, ministry, fund-raising, or sales promotional use. For information, please email info@EllieClaire.com.

Edited by Barbara Farmer
Cover and interior design by Gearbox | studiogearbox.com

Printed in China

1 2 3 4 5 6 7 8 9 – 21 20 19 18 17 16

About the Author

As the mother of a former frontline infantry Marine, Edie Melson understands what it is to face adversity and come out triumphant on the other side. Her years as a wife, mother, and ministry leader have given her a unique perspective to reach out to others facing the same struggles. She's the Military Family Blogger for Guideposts.org, social media director for several writing Web sites, and a popular ministry and conference speaker. She lives in Simpsonville, South Carolina.